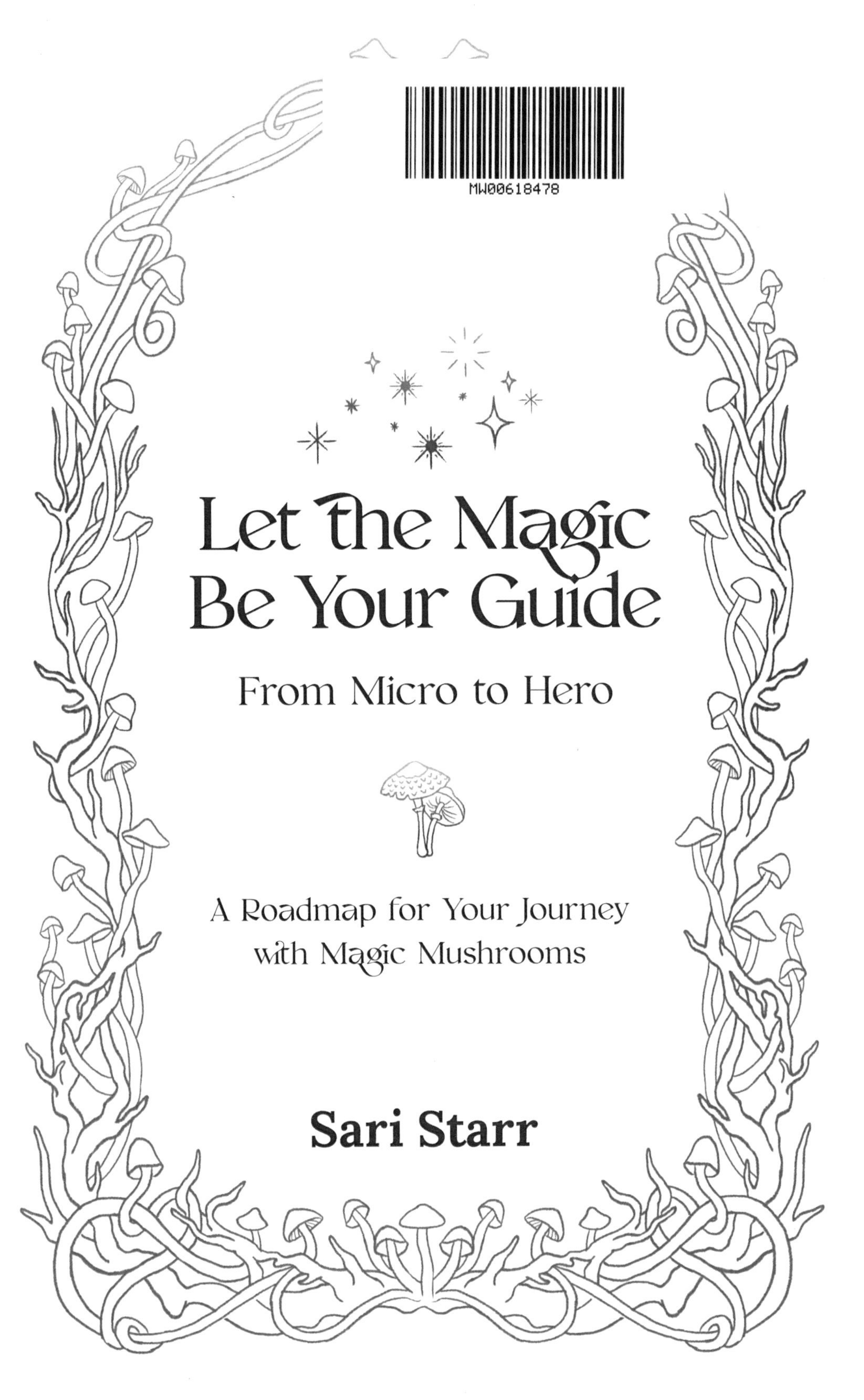

Let the Magic Be Your Guide

From Micro to Hero

A Roadmap for Your Journey with Magic Mushrooms

Sari Starr

Starrseed Enterprises LLC
www.saristarr.com
www.celestialsmokes.com

Disclaimer:
Nothing in this guide should be taken as medical advice, advice for healing, nor am I condoning in any way the use of any substances without guidance, or a licensed professional. This book is being used as a blueprint should you, the reader, want to explore psilocybin on your own, you have a tool to assist you by offering a road map to a safe journey.

ISBN: 978-0-578-93689-5

Illustrations by ZIYA
Cover and book design by Christine Lee
Editing Contributors: Keith Hodder and Brenna Kischuk
Research Contributor: Carlos Zabarain
Content Contributor: Galyn Burke, Licensed Therapist
Printed and bound in the USA

As our society gets more and more interested in psychedelics and specifically psilocybin, information and destigmatization become crucial in providing harm reduction to the people who wish to venture in these complex territories. Sari's book offers well-organized and useful support and orientation as she diligently speaks of intention, preparation, care and caution, and integration. I am pleased to see such writings come into people's hands for safe and fruitful experiences.

—Françoise Bourzat

Author of *Consciousness Medicine* and Founder of The Center for Consciousness Medicine

www.centerforcm.com

This medicine is a spiritual experience. One must be in such a mindset to experience its healing properties. This guide did just that! The mantras definitely put you in the right space to begin any journey, reminding you why and what you should take away from your journey. The other tips and explanations helped me so much, as I am new to this medicine.

—Chris

Sari's insight and guidance with the medicine is profound and beautifully provoking. She has guided me to heal my life and relationships in ways I assumed were not possible.

—Sunny G.

Sari's guidance through the realms of plant medicine journeys has had a profound impact on my life. Her wisdom is deep and the way she guides each being to commune with the plant kingdom offers a transformational opportunity that I'm deeply grateful to have received.

—Greyson

Contents

CHAPTER ONE

Welcome

As humans, we are conditioned to believe that our reality is a product of our experience. We tend to believe we are a direct manifestation of our external environment, status, title, bank account, and our overall perceived identity. This is a modern day narrative to keep us disconnected from our true nature. The more disconnected we are, the more we consume and identify with what we are not.

However, as we become more aware and dive deeper into our vast innerverse, we have the opportunity to shift our awareness and quantum leap into our unlimited potential freeing ourselves from limiting beliefs that prevent us from experiencing our true power and supernatural abilities.

We begin to understand that reality and truth comes from **within**. We can unlock it by taking a journey that our Spirit has been aching to take. A journey that generations have taken before us to discover the meaning of our existence as well as our soul's individual and collective purpose.

It's a rite of passage, one firmly entrenched in the human experience and plucked from the grounding Earth beneath our feet. It's our odyssey.

Many think that psychedelics are a trend of the "new age," but the earliest humans took their own journeys using the same plants. In fact, ancient practices guided by master medicine teachers and shamans used magic mushrooms, cannabis, ayahuasca, and mescaline. These plants are rooted in the primordial lineage that dates all the way back to the beginnings of our species, and according to Paul Stamets, potentially played a significant role in our evolution as a species. More on this in the history section.

Today, many have forgotten their roots and lost themselves along the way, the practice of a spiritual journey has diminished greatly over decades, resulting in generations plagued by anxiety and ancestral trauma. Only now, amids the psychedelic renaissance, is our spiritual awakening resurrected. A new era of conscious awareness and self-actualization is upon us.

Many can attribute this to our call back to plant-based medicinal entheogens, offering the collective an opportunity to face our lineage of wounding and free our minds from mental enslavement to the ego, or self. Psychedelics hold the keys that unlock the many gateways to understanding and experiencing our true essence beyond form. When we experience ourselves in our energetic bodies we begin to feel love in ways that have been foreign and forgotten in this physical form. As a result of this ecstatic phenomena, it is natural for us to want to embody this state of awareness on a regular basis. This is where we have seen the radical shift from living in a state of suffering and pain to a state of acceptance and joy. For some it is a journey straight into the womb of the Great Mother, pure childlike bliss and love, and for others it is a path into the dark night of the soul which can be a challenging process to unveil. Yet, no matter how we get there our goal and the goal of these medicines is to guide us home, acting as a quantum compass into the depths of existence, so we can truly remember our Divine Nature unity consciousness and love.

In this guide we will explore how to use Magic Mushrooms in an intentional and beneficial way. Whether we are feeling called to microdose, journey, fly solo or in a group, these pages will prepare you to embark on an adventure that will transform life as you know it.

As you read this guide, I invite you to empty all your thoughts, all your preconceived ideas, expectations, desires, and fears. See yourself as an empty vessel and a clear transmission for the true wisdom to come through, because once you decide to commune with these Plant-Medicines the journey has already begun.

Welcome to the first step of your journey.

María Sabina

Photo credit: www.elmaestrocompentente.blogspot.com/2021/03/María-sabina.html

CHAPTER TWO

A Brief History of Mushrooms

Stone paintings from the Saharan Aboriginal Tribes of North Africa suggest the use of mushrooms as far back as 9,000 B.C. Similarly, rock paintings in Spain from about 6,000 years ago offer glimpses into religious rituals where mushrooms were potentially used. Comparable evidence has been uncovered in the remnants of Native American and Aztec communities as well. The writing is on the wall.

Fast forward to 1955 when the Oaxacan village of Huautla is recorded as the location of the first ever shamanistic mushroom experience. George Wasson, a former New York banker and hobbyist mycologist, landed in the small native town of the Mixeteco tribe after a thirty year search for the divine mushrooms.

It was there that he met well-respected healer and shaman María Sabina who had been consuming psilocybin mushrooms since the age of seven. The night she met Wasson, she performed a ceremony she had been practicing for decades, and one that would ultimately change his life forever. After a potent night of communing with the highly visual and intense mushrooms, or "saint children's (Ninios) medicine" as María called them, Wasson returned home to tell his story. In 1957, he published his account in LIFE Magazine, entitled "Seeking the Magic Mushroom," which described his experience. The article rapidly caught the attention of the American public and lit the fuse of the psychedelic counterculture (source: www.timeline.com).

CHAPTER THREE

Dosing Suggestions

There are **four** common dosing protocols you can follow, each differing significantly in experience: microdose, low dose, journey, and Hero's dose It is important to understand how to dose appropriately so that you don't end up on a trip with the wrong intention and setting, or plan for a big journey and come up short.

These protocols will help you understand what to expect in order to plan your experience around them. The main thing to consider is that every person is unique and has different sensitivities, so a low dose could be like a micro for some people and a journey for others.

Because the science and research is limited, it is always recommended to start slowly and discover your sensitivities to the Plant-Medicine to ensure you are protected and feel safe enough to fully surrender to your experience. Much like cannabis, there are various different strains of mushrooms which we will cover some more later on. Depending on how they are grown and the many variables in the process from inoculation to fruit, strength and potency of the strain will vary. Generally, the psilocybin strains have similar effects and you can get a sense of your dose from self-experimentation. You are your own case study and this guide is a blueprint, but the real understanding will come from your own experiences. If you plan on consuming them in raw form, this would be a great time to buy a scale.

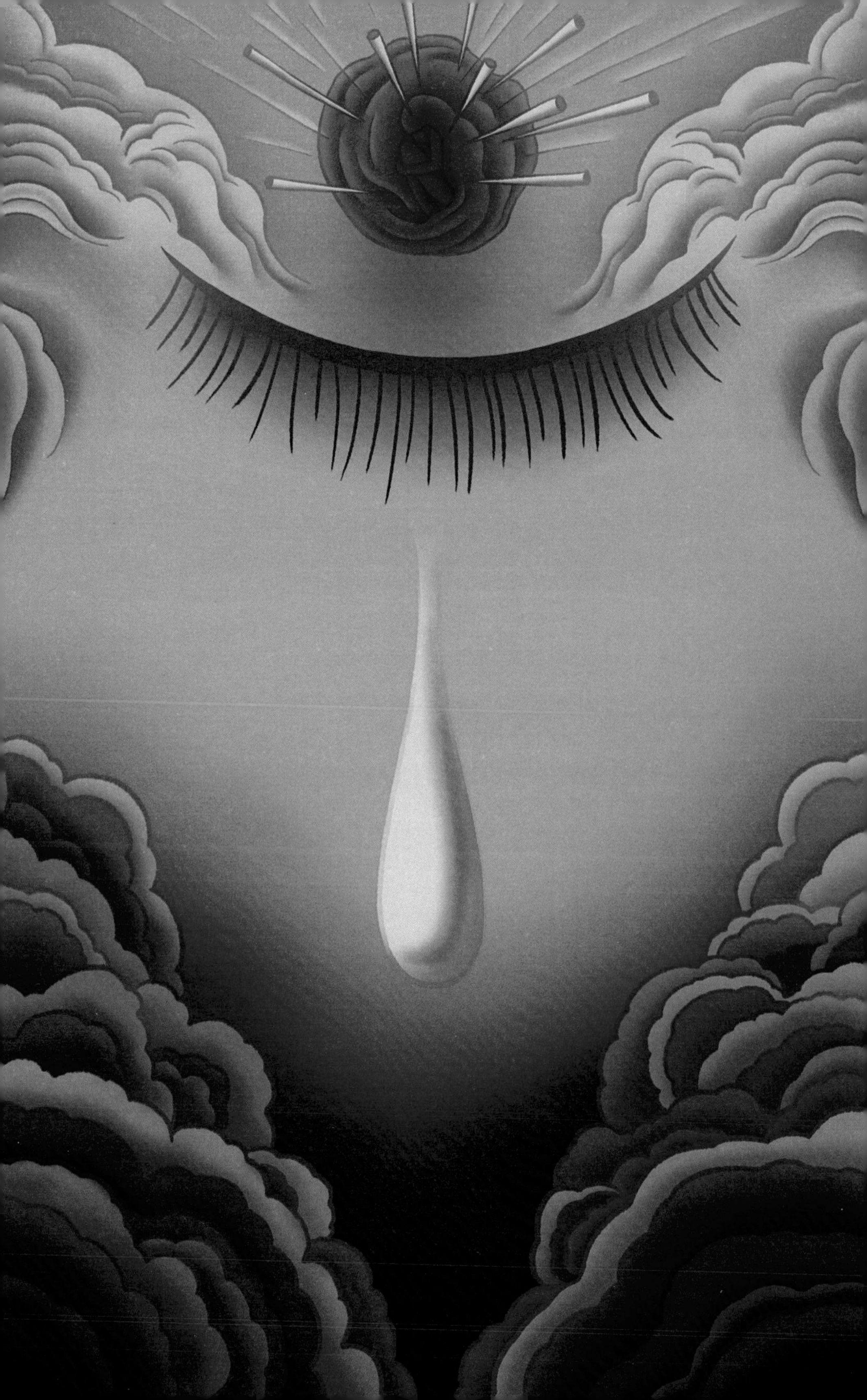

Microdose

A microdose is exactly that, a micro amount of a full dose (The Journey). It typically ranges from 0.1g to 0.3g. People generally take microdoses and continue to be high-functioning and even enhanced-functioning throughout the day. A micro can give you a lot of energy and focus, as well as offer a sense of peace and well-being, allowing you to handle stressful situations with ease.

Most anyone can benefit from microdosing, and most research talks about people using it to manage anxiety, depression, and PTSD. Keep in mind that the majority of the articles are focused on medical use, as that is paving the way to legalization.

People who are interested in expanding their consciousness, their brain function, their focus, creativity, energy, libido, and joy are great candidates for microdosing. It is often an ally for movement activities and can even enhance your performance. People like to microdose at festivals, clubs, ecstatic dance, yoga, and meditation.

Microdosing Protocols

There are a few well-known protocols developed by the top researchers of psilocybin. According to *Psychedelic's Daily*, here's a protocol you can follow:

Microdose every day for general cognitive enhancement.	Microdose every weekday with weekends off for business and professional work-life enhancement.	Microdose every other day for psychological management of anxiety, depression, PTSD, etc.

According to Dr. James Fadiman, the leading researcher on microdosing effects of LSD and psilocybin mushrooms, this is how to enjoy your first week of microdosing:

DAY 01	DAY 02	DAY 03	DAY 04
Dose, feel the effects, and keep a journal of everything you do and how you feel.	The effects are still present, but they are not as pronounced.	Effects noticeably absent. This is a day of rest and comparison/ contrast.	Dose again.

Dr. Fadiman's recommendations for self-study are ideal because it gives you a chance to see what's going on. After one month—an ideal test-period—most people say that they're still microdosing, but not as often (source: *Psychedelic's Daily*).

Paul Stamets has a protocol recommendation of:

- 1-10mg psilocybin/psilocin
- 200-500mg lion's mane mushroom extract
- 101-200mg niacin

The protocol calls for taking this stack five times in a row and then two days off. It is important to note that a 0.1g of psilocybin will likely not be felt, and niacin can create a niacin flush, which is a flushing of blood to the face, causing redness and uncomfortable sensations (*Nootropedia*, 2019).

There are benefits to mixing psilocybin mushrooms with non-psychoactive adaptogen mushrooms, as is recommended in Paul's protocol. Mushrooms possess a lot of health benefits in general, and if this is something that beckons your curiosity there is the opportunity to dive deeper into the world of medicinal mushroom benefits.

This is a great opportunity to use your intuition. You will know when you are in need of a dose and when you are not. The best person to guide you is you and your connection to the medicine.

Entry Level Dose

A low dose is around 1–2 grams depending on your sensitivity. Many people take this dose when they want to gain some insight into their inner wisdom with less mind chatter. While this arena doesn't dissolve your ego fully, it does offer an opportunity to connect deeper with your heart and with that the ability to calm the mind and tap into your intuition.

This is a great dose when you want to be still for a few hours, meditate, write, brainstorm, and of course explore nature alone or with some close friends. This is also a nice dose for an outdoor festival or dance party, though this is cautioned for a newbie. It is recommended that your first time be in a safe, calm, and quiet environment, and to follow the protocols outlined in this guide for a self-guided or group journey.

Typically when people take these doses (and higher), it's best they surround themselves with others who are also partaking. When we enter into the "field" of mushrooms, we tend to want people around us who understand what we are experiencing and observe reality from similar perspectives. The lens of reality greatly shifts and if you are connecting with someone who is not on the same vibe, it can be somewhat of a buzzkill. The exception is someone who is experienced in mushroom trips and can hold space in a way that allows them access to this field without the medicine.

First time users who want to experience mushrooms could start with this dose. Some people want to dip their toes in the water by starting with a microdose; however, in my opinion (which varies case by case) the sooner we dive into the abyss of the unknown and learn how to let go and surrender to trust, the sooner we find rapid growth and transformation. This dose allows us to feel the mushrooms and understand how they work more intricately. A microdose serves a much different purpose than an entry level or journey, and the connection and feeling with the medicine is significantly different as well. The purpose of microdosing is a gentle subconscious rewiring, offering up a general feeling of well-being which can reprogram the mind over time. Alternatively, a mid to high-level dose will throw us into the abyss of change and allow us to begin a new relationship with who we think we are.

That's not to say that starting with a microdose as your first time is wrong. There is no right or wrong way to build a relationship with mushrooms. The only way is your personal way, and this guide acts as a companion to your own intuition and experience so that you may journey safely with the most rewarding outcomes.

The Journey

The Journey is between 2–4grams, leaning towards the 3–4g range. This is an experience where you may begin to see visuals, and where you can dive deep into discovering insightful wisdom. Many enjoy "The Journey" surrounded by nature, inside, or in ceremony with others. The ceremonial instructions in this guide are designed for doses 1.5g and above.

With this dose, most (if not all) of our ego is dissolved and we can look at our life from the perspective of heart-knowing, or our higher-self. We are able to see all the ways we experience our emotions and challenges without the self-criticism, judgment, fear, or attachment to a specific outcome. An internal dialogue is common, and in some cases, we may hear voices from what seem to be like "other beings." Many people have been contacted by extraterrestrials, deceased loved ones, deities, and different archetypes. No journey is the same, which makes each experience an opportunity to surrender to the unknown.

It is important that when we start to feel the mushrooms take effect that we fully allow the experience to reveal itself without trying to resist or fight against it. How we achieve this primarily consists of allowing whatever shows up to reveal itself without pushing it away from our psyche or trying to make sense of it with the mind.

It is best to see yourself as the observer, as though you are watching a movie about your life and the character you play on this earth. Trust that you are getting what you need and do not be attached to any outcome (*I cannot stress this part enough*). The one thing that you can be certain of is that if you set the proper intentions and settings, the mushrooms will give you exactly what you need to know. There are many times that you will pose a question and receive direct guidance from your inner voice; however, there are also times where that question will not be answered in the moment. Don't be frustrated, just continue to trust the process. All will be revealed in Divine Timing, whether it is during, immediately, or long after the journey. This experience is the gift that will keep on giving if you continue to connect with the energy and do the necessary integration work required to unpack this Divine Wisdom.

Hero's Dose

The "heroic dose" is a term coined by Terrence McKenna, one of the founding pioneers of psychedelic research and experimentation, which is 5g or more of dried psilocybin mushrooms. The thought behind this is that in order for a person to have a profound breakthrough, one must dive into the abyss and break the threshold of all egoic obstacles.

When working with mushrooms in all doses they can help gain insight into childhood trauma, recover lost memories, access emotions, and deepen insights into your life in review. According to McKenna, taking the heroic dose gets us to the "bullseye of the mandala" that is the psychedelic experience.

What happens there, is a shattering of our current reality and a blastoff into realms that are beyond anything we could ever imagine or fully comprehend. McKenna believes that this dosage should be taken less often, a few times a year, and that processing the information and experience could take a significant amount of time. He also recommends taking it in quiet darkness so that the entire experience is a fully inward one, and a complete surrender to the unknown.

While many people have journeyed with this dose, it depends on the sensitivity of the individual, as sometimes people do not need a full 5g to enter this state of awareness with the mushrooms. Unless you are a seasoned psychonaut, it is highly recommended that you do this dose with a trip sitter, in a ceremony or with a trained guide. Mushrooms are an intense master teacher and sometimes the journey can feel unpleasant and challenging as we get ready to face our fears, the unknown aspects of our existence, and the deepest parts of ourselves.

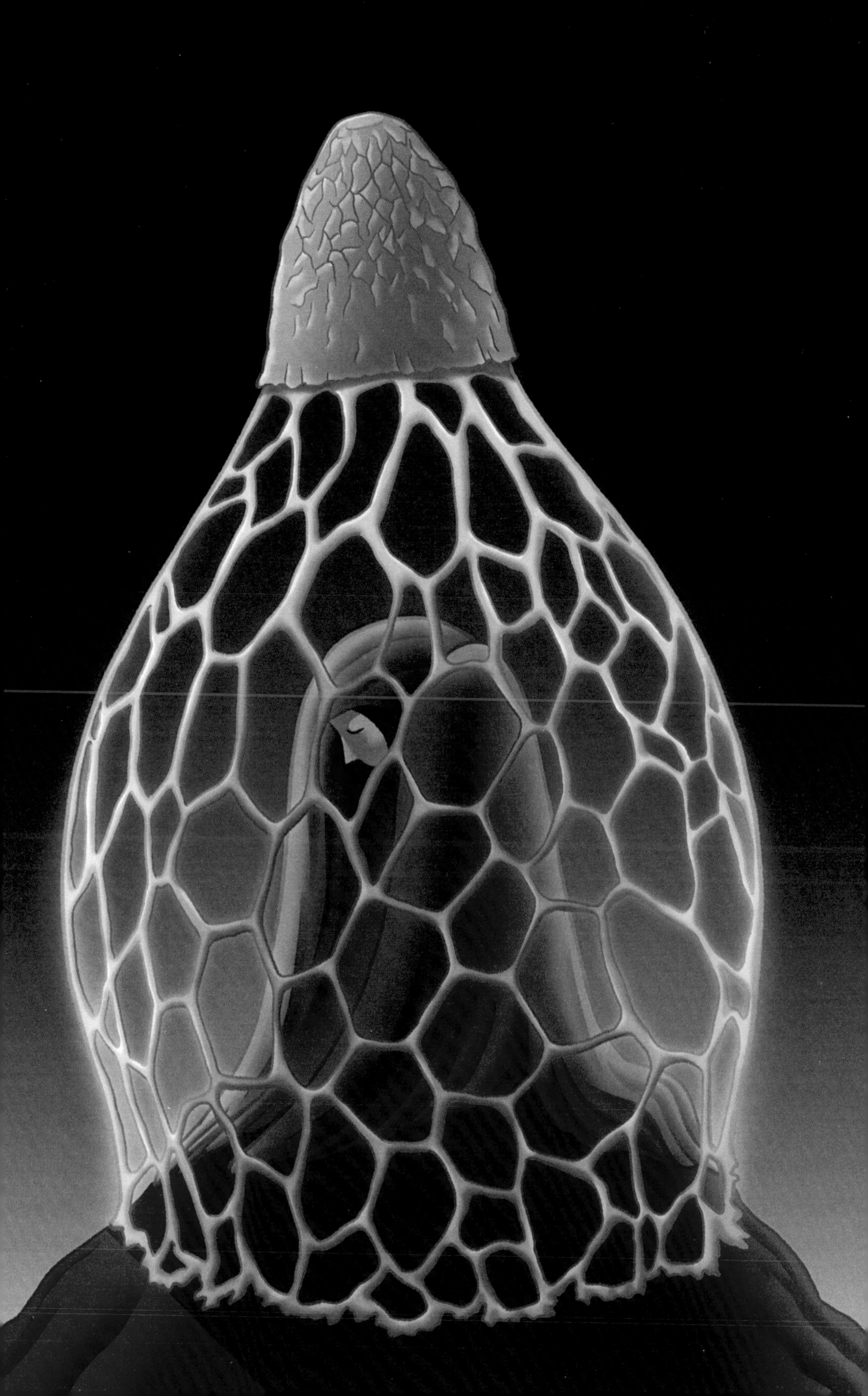

The "Bad Trip"

When you begin your journey with any Plant-Medicine, it is normal to desire an outcome that will be perceived as "positive."

Many have heard the term "bad trip," which creates fear and stigma around connecting with this medicine. **It is important to understand that there is no negative outcome from any journey.** If you create the proper environment, intention, and protocol, you will be able to receive any challenges with more ease and understanding.

As mentioned earlier, mushrooms will give you exactly what you need to see and know. Sometimes those things are buried traumas, emotions, and memories. Before you allow these emotions to take over, it is possible to shift your perspective and embrace this as a clear indication of what needs to be released.

This is why it is **ideal** to have someone with you who knows how to support you in a challenging situation. However, if you feel courageous and do not have the ability to have an assist, facilitator or ceremonialist, here are a few ways you can learn to navigate your experience and move through it to the other side:

If you start to see distorted images, or feel unsettled or uncomfortable, surrender to the feeling and accept that this is the experience you are having, without wanting it to change. This will allow you to observe and learn what the mushrooms are teaching you. The more you try to "escape," the harder the experience will be. Be aware and focus on your breath. You can also put your hand on your heart and focus on its natural rhythm. You can start saying a mantra that you find healing (as recommended below in **Guiding Your Intentions**).

If you submit yourself to the experience, the medicine will show you what needs to be explored from a place of calm observation. Please keep in mind that you are here to learn about your authentic self. The more we learn about how to access our heart-knowing, the better equipped we will be when challenging moments arise. There is nothing to fear when you take the time to build this relationship responsibly.

A great way to calm our nervous system is to move the energy out of our body. Running in place, jumping jacks, dancing, or any form of quick cardio will help bring you back to a calmer state. This is usually an option with a lower dose; in a higher dose it is typically hard for us to move as our body can feel heavy and almost paralyzed.

If movement is not an option for you, releasing sound through grunting, yelling, singing, chanting and crying helps. Whenever you feel uncomfortable in a medicine journey, it is usually the time where you may feel the need to purge stuck energy. Crying can be very cathartic and healing. Sometimes you will have to visit the bathroom. Yawning is another form of purging. All forms of energy release will allow you to move the restrictive programming from your cells and reprogram your association with your past.

The most important thing you can do is recognize that you are the observer of your mental-movie. You can always return to love by placing your hand on your heart and reciting your mantra.

What you resist persists, so rather than fighting against yourself, allow the energy of your emotions to arise and use this as an opportunity to begin your conversation with the mushrooms, your higher-self, and ultimately love.

The most important thing you can do is recognize that you are the observer of your mental-movie.

CHAPTER FOUR

Species & Types of Psilocybin Mushrooms

The Psilocybe genus, the main class of psilocybin mushrooms are composed of over 200 species. The four most prevalent of these are Azurescens, Semilanceata, Cubensis, and Cyanescens, but there are hundreds of species included in the genus. (**www.psilopedia.com/) All species of Psilocybe mushroom are visually differing, and contain varying levels of psychoactive compounds (primarily psilocybin, psilocin, baeocystin and norbaeocystin). Different species also produce subtly varied psychotropic effects.

Psilocybe Cubensis is arguably the most common and popular species of magic mushrooms because of their easy growth ability and identifiable characteristics. There now exist over 60 distinct Psilocybe Cubensis "strains" or "types." It is interesting to note that fungi are more similar to the human genome than to the plant genome, and we consist of more fungus than cells. Additionally, fungi are very much like humans; they inhale oxygen and exhale CO_2.

Some of the more popular strains found today are:

Ecuadorian	B+	Pink Buffalo
Albino A+	Mekechanii	Liberty Caps
Penis Envy	Golden Teachers	Hawaiian
Aztech	Cambodian	Guadalajara

CHAPTER FIVE

Methods of Consumption

There are a handful of methods to consume mushrooms: raw and fresh, raw and dried, in a tea or a hot drink, and cooked or baked in other food (typically chocolate). The way mushrooms are consumed have a direct impact on the potency and duration of the experience.

It is important to know the source of your mushrooms to ensure the integrity of the grow and quality. It is also beneficial to own a mini scale to know the exact dose you are taking.

Fresh

When consuming fresh mushrooms, you want to make sure that you eat them shortly after being picked, and/or store them in a paper bag in the fridge. After about a week they will begin to mold and possibly lose their potency. Generally, fresh mushrooms can be a little stronger than the dried ones.

Dried

Dried mushrooms are a more typical method of consumption due to their long shelf-life. Eating raw mushrooms can be known to cause stomach aches and/or nausea. It's good to keep some mint tea close by as an option to offset some potential stomach discomfort. This is less frequent with microdosing. Also, some people are genetically predisposed and are Dried mushrooms are a more typical method of consumption due to their long shelf-life. Eating raw mushrooms can be known to cause stomach aches and/or nausea. It's good to keep some mint tea close by as an option to offset some potential stomach discomfort. This is less frequent with microdosing. Also, some people are genetically predisposed and are unable to stomach mushrooms, though this is rare. When we discuss the dosing protocols we are referring to dried weight. Make sure that the mushrooms are dried enough that they feel brittle and can snap in half; this will ensure you are getting the accurate weight per dose, as mushrooms that are not fully dried still carry water and this will throw off the dose ratio to the weight.

Baked or Cooked

In addition to potential stomach upset, many find the Earthly taste of raw mushrooms to be "off-putting." This is why people like to consume their mushrooms in chocolate form. When prepared correctly, mixing high-end cacao and mushrooms with other high-quality ingredients can actually enhance the experience as well as the flavor.

Cacao is also known to be a heart-opener (meaning it helps you access a more natural, loving state) and stimulant, which can activate the mushrooms quicker with a more intense journey. Cacao is also an MAOI inhibitor which can elongate and amplify the effects psilocybin has on the brain. Adding additional adaptogen mushrooms can also increase potency, offering benefits to overall health and brain function. Some examples of adaptogen mushrooms are: Reishi, Cordyceps, Lion's Mane, Shiitake, etc.

Tea or Hot Drink

Drinking mushroom tea is a potential way to mitigate the stomach-ache effects of psilocybin. It bypasses the liver and is easier on the digestive system. When drinking tea the onset of the effects are typically quicker, but in some cases the journey is shorter, As with everything mentioned in this guide, each individual's experience is different and varies from person to person.

Tea Preparation Instructions:

- Boil water.
- Wait 7 minutes.
- Steep mushrooms for 15 minutes (you can add other teas and honey for taste).
- Drink within 5 minutes (do not sip over a long period of time, you want to consume the medicine all at once for a proper dose)
- You can also steep them in a warm cacao drink.

Alternatives

Research is being done on the process of extracting psilocin, the active ingredient that psilocybin converts into to create its mind-altering effects. Like making mushroom tea, this has the potential to eliminate stomach distress. This will lead to more exploration on how to properly dose based on the specific extraction methods, and will likely be more potent than consuming in the natural raw form. As research becomes more available and more case studies are reported, there will be more consistent conclusions to the direct effects of consuming Plant-Medicine in general. Currently some methods of extraction include soaking them in a base like honey or various other chemical extraction methods.

CHAPTER SIX

Mixing Substances

As a general rule, mixing psychoactive substances should be done under supervision or with someone experienced. That said, if you are completely new to mushrooms, it is recommended that you try them on their own first to explore the various methods of dosage and consumption and begin to form a relationship. That way you'll understand your limits and tolerance before mixing substances.

Slow and steady is always best. If you are deep in the medicine, it's best to allow the medicine to work with you without adding any additional stimulants. Oftentimes you can ask the medicine (or your higher-self) if you need something else and you will get the answer that will serve your best experience.

Preferably, you will enter into a mushroom ceremony without any previous substances and receive the desired effect without needing to enhance it. There are certain times where some medicines mixed together may serve a valuable purpose.

It's important to understand the timing of mixing substances, as each has different effects on the outcome: **Disclaimer:** I am not promoting mixing any substances, however given that this is common throughout social culture, this guide offers a safer exploration in doing so.

Cannabis:

- Only recommended if you don't feel the effects of the mushrooms enough or if it's taking longer than usual to hit (over one hour if eaten over 30 min if consumed as tea).
- **A little goes a long way.** Start with 1–2 puffs. Cannabis is an activator, so it is unlikely to feel high from it because it triggers and enhances the substance ingested prior to smoking.
- **Don't take an edible.** It will take too long to kick in and you may find yourself on a journey hours longer and later than you've prepared for.
- **Smoking is the best method of consumption** as it is the fastest bioavailability through the lungs and it does not have to bypass the liver through digestion.
- Cannabis before mushrooms is okay. It makes the journey a little more intense.
- If you feel the mushrooms are enough, you may want to wait a few hours to enjoy a nice joint and use it as your integration tool. Cannabis can elongate the light mushroom effects towards the end of the journey, allowing you to reflect and write while maintaining the altered state of awareness.

Cacao:

- Cacao contains small amounts of enzyme inhibitors, called MAO inhibitors, that are capable of slowing the breakdown of the psychoactive compounds found in mushrooms to perpetuate or amplify the effects. Not only in combination with mushrooms, but when consumed alone cacao remains a very chemically complex food with both mind and body-altering effects.
- You can steep mushrooms in cacao instead of tea.
- You can eat mushrooms in the form of chocolate.
- You can drink it before or after your ceremony.
- It adds a beautiful layer of softness to your experience.
- It offers health benefits when using microdose chocolates and can mitigate the bitter taste of the raw mushrooms.

Tobacco:

- Tobacco has been traditionally used as a sacred medicine by native and indigenous cultures. It's used to pray and clear energies, originally shared in sweat ceremonies.
- **Cigarettes are not recommended.**
- When using pure, organic tobacco in a prayerful and ceremonial way, it's best to roll your own tobacco in a corn husk, however rolling paper—such as hemp works fine.
- Tobacco is normally used to open a ceremony with a prayer of intention. When praying with tobacco, the smoke is NOT inhaled. It is offered to the spirits so that the prayer lifts and is received with the pure smoke.
- If you would like to enjoy your tobacco and inhale, do so towards the end of the journey when medicine is not strong. Sometimes tobacco can cause lightheadedness, head rush or even nausea when on medicine. Be gentle with inhales, taking one or two, and wait to see how your body reacts before continuing.
- Tobacco can bring down the "high" of the mushrooms and ground you back into your body
- Hapé—a form of tobacco snuff that is used in ceremonial settings, typically administered by a shaman or facilitator. It can also be self administered by people who are experienced, and helps to ground and bring you out of the altered state. This can be a good way to connect to the spirit of tobacco before consuming mushrooms, or when the sensation of medicine is no longer strong.

MDMA

- Some people do what is called a "hippy flip," mixing a microdose of MDMA and a microdose of mushrooms. The effect is usually euphoric, and offers heightened awareness and energy, as well as feelings of love and joy.

- People typically take a hippy flip before dancing. It can enhance your social experience, alleviate any social discomfort and allow you to be more honed into your heart and body.
- **Make sure that you test your MDMA** to ensure it's of pure quality. Even reliable sources can have impurities in the pills and this can lead to adverse effects with or without mushrooms.
- Because you are mixing a chemical with a plant-medicine, it's critical to recognize that there is a chance it doesn't balance with your own personal brain chemistry. **Proceed with caution**—chemicals are a lot more dangerous than working with nature.

Alcohol

- **NOT RECOMMENDED.** Especially in a ceremony setting.
- Alcohol holds a very different vibration and frequency than Plant-Medicine and it has a VERY different effect on your brain.
- Mixing mushrooms is not advisable as it can cause adverse reactions which can be harmful.
- This has bad repercussions beyond just yourself. When people use plants irresponsibly and mix it with alcohol and something bad happens, it emphasizes the stigma and hurts all the progress we have done to date.

Psychiatric Medications

Because mushrooms and psychotropic medications like SSRI's engage the same receptors in our brains, the chronic use of antidepressants and other psychiatric medications can alter the effects of mushrooms, impact dosage and lead to some unsafe interactions in the brain and body. Thus, if you're taking any medications, but especially anti-anxiety or antidepressant medications, you should consult with a healthcare professional before working with the mushroom.[1]

—***Galyn Burke,*** Licensed Family & Marriage Therapist

CHAPTER SEVEN

What to Expect From Your Experience

There are typically **four phases** of the journey: the onset, the peak, the come down, and the integration period.

Onset can occur within 30 mins to an hour of ingesting, depending on the method of consumption. It typically feels like you're slowing down significantly. Your body gets heavy, you may feel waves of nausea, and there is a feeling of leaving this reality, similar to sleep paralysis (a state in which a person is aware they are in a dream/sleep state but unable to move or speak). **The onset typically lasts about 30 mins to an hour.**

The peak comes next. It can feel like you've slipped into a trance state, similar to waking dreams. Senses are heightened and emotions are elevated, whether pleasant or challenging.

This is the time to surrender to the experience and allow the guidance of the mushrooms to take you on your journey. You may hear a voice communicating with you in your head, guiding you. You may see or connect with non-physical beings and feel the presence of deceased loved ones.

This is often the most intense part of the journey and the opportunity to study your thoughts, life experiences, and beliefs from a perspective of presence, all while your ego takes a back seat. **The peak can last from two to four hours.**

The come down is unlike hard party substances. The end of this experience doesn't leave you wanting more or feeling low. It's a gentle and smooth transition as you slowly begin to come back to your body and full sense of self. You will likely feel very mellow, at peace and aligned with your thoughts and emotions. If you had a challenging experience you may feel exhausted and a little distraught, but allow all emotions and feelings to come through and be present with them; the work of integrating your experience is just beginning.

You may still feel a little unbalanced and uncoordinated. Do not drive until you've had a good amount of rest. It is perfectly normal to feel exhausted but have trouble falling asleep. If so, be patient. At some point you will get a comforting and well earned rest.

Integration is the most important phase of the process. It is the time to reflect and unpack the entire experience piece-by-piece. This will allow you to discover and interpret the meaning of everything that was revealed.

This is a good time to make a journal entry expressing everything you felt, saw, and heard throughout your journey. This is important to note that this process of "unpacking" can take days, weeks, months, or even years! The learning we receive from our mushroom experiences offers us ongoing insight and long lasting benefits as we re-integrate into our lives with a newfound awareness, noticing significant differences to our behavioral patterns. We often surprise ourselves at our ability to be less reactive, stressed, and triggered by things that would have challenged us in the past. These pleasant discoveries are just one indication of the true life-affirming benefits that our connection with Plant-Medicines, in this case mushrooms, can offer.

CHAPTER EIGHT

Preparing for the Journey

Plant-Medicines can enhance many experiences. Your senses will be heightened, so preparing a safe and welcoming space will contribute to receiving the most beneficial outcome from your inward journey.

These experiences open up your energy field and amplify your intuitive connection, especially if you are already sensitive, empathic, and/or psychic.

During this experience be aware that you are working for your own growth and for the collective. This is a big part of sitting in a ceremonial and intentional frequency, we learn how to return to the ONE, to Source, and we begin to remember that we are all truly connected.

Since this is a self-guided experience, there are a few key elements to create an environment that is supportive and freeing. Fill your space and surroundings with items, textures and smells that inspire you and bring you joy. Remove anything that aggravates you or stimulates aggression or anxiety.

Here's a helpful checklist:

- Make sure your space does not have any outside distractions or disturbances. (people, social media, loud noises, abrupt visitors, etc.).
- Have a conversation with anyone you're living with so they understand and give you the space you need. Ensure that your requirements are clearly communicated.
- Let your family know that you will not be available to them. Help them understand that you will need your own uninterrupted space and that you may behave in unfamiliar or unexpected ways.
- Make sure you are comfortable and relaxed whether you are inside or outside.
- Sage yourself and the space to clear any unwanted energies. Incense and candles definitely enhance relaxation.
- The choice of music you listen to is important. It's best to avoid any music that has nostalgic reference to past events taking you out of the present moment.
- Choose a good playlist ahead of time so you are not concerned about the next song. During the Mushroom journey make sure your playlist lasts at least 4–6 hours, with no commercial breaks, and your phone/speakers are plugged in and charged. It is best to have it programmed to play on repeat.
  Sari's Medicine Playlist: https://soundcloud.com/cannabispriestess/sets/medicine-music
  East Forest Magic Mushrooms: https://open.spotify.com/album/4IoMVqRAfQgdD43RCDx4r1?si=3lVi zp0fSkm_UhbijoUK3A
- Turn your phone to airplane mode and download the music you're playing. Avoid mid-journey interruptions such as the ending of music, battery dying, commercials, etc.
- Make sure the climate is comfortable and you have layers you can remove or add, as body temperature sometimes fluctuates. With mushrooms, people tend to run cold.

- If you enjoy working with crystals you may want to have them near you.
- Keep a journal next to you, so you can write down your thoughts.
- Essential oils can help activate the senses and the plants you choose can definitely participate in your experience to enhance the journey.
- Have a mantra to repeat that helps you stay calm. I recommend Ho'ponopono the Hawaiian forgiveness mantra. It is extremely powerful when facing challenging situations. "*Please Forgive me, Thank you, I love you.*"
- A few other helpful Mantras (repeat them):
    1. *I AM loving awareness*
    2. *Om Gam Ganapataye Namaha (remover of obstacles)*
    3. *I am safe I am loved*
    4. *I remember who I AM*
    5. *Chanting the Primordial* "OMMMM"
    6. *Please show me the way home with ease and grace*
- Remember in any challenging moment to always come back to love.
- Surround yourself with pillows, blankets, water, and snacks (typically during a mushroom journey you won't want to eat, but it's always nice to have the option).
- Have a delicious light meal prepared for when you are finished.
- Pets are good to have around if they are generally calm. Make sure they are fed and walked before you begin.

It's recommended you go on a journey that will allow you to truly surrender to the experience. Depending on how sensitive and experienced you are, **a typical dose is between 2–3g**. This will allow you to break the threshold and dive deeper into your authentic self beyond the interference of the ego. The length of this journey will last about 5–6 hours.

CHAPTER NINE

Guiding Your Intentions

Whether you've come to the beginning of this journey with excitement, curiosity, fear, or a combination of many feelings and thoughts, preparation is key.

Think about it. It would be unwise to go camping without equipment, a map, a plan. And while this is a trip that can be safely taken from the comfort of your home, a plan is still needed—a mental one. Your state of being when you consume Plant-Medicines is vital.

Mushrooms can amplify what you're already feeling and depend on many variables, such as: dosing, method of consumption, strains, and your individual metabolism and DNA. It is important to experiment with different products and strains until you find the one that supports your personal experience the most.

Part of this journey is learning to trust and guide yourself. As soon as you decide to work with the mushrooms it is advisable to focus on your intentions without expectations. This will help create an energetic and mental connection to work with nature's wisdom keepers. One thing you will learn is that the physical form is only one aspect of how we communicate, connect, and manifest.

As soon as we decide on a path, the energy of that decision already begins to manifest. This is one of the powerful ways we can gain awareness around designing our best life.

Before you begin a ceremony, you may want to say or meditate on the following to bring awareness to your commitment, and soothe your expectations:

- "*I lay all expectations at the door.*"
- "*I am open to receiving any and all communication from the medicine as I am aware that this is all for me to witness my true self and go beyond the ego mind.*"
- "*I am here for the greater good of the collective and to be of service to my higher-self.*"
- "*I am aware that the only true teacher here is my own inner wisdom and the plants and facilitators are guides to help me access that wisdom in a meaningful way.*"
- "*I am entering into this field free from all outside distractions that pull me away from this ceremonial circle, which includes social media, TV, news, and people who do not serve my highest vibration.*"
- "*I understand that everyone is on their own journey and I respect each person's personal boundaries while I'm in ceremony with others.*"
- "*I will lead with kindness and compassion for myself and others.*"
- "*I will be active and present from beginning to end and I understand that this medicine is sacred.*"
- "I AM HERE NOW."

CHAPTER TEN

Steps to Begin Your Communication With Plant-Medicine

Now that you've learned the proper dosage, methods of consumption, and have prepared yourself for the journey and know what to expect, it's time to embark:

- Close your eyes and breathe deeply.
- Start paying attention to your body. Go intently into areas that are rarely explored; your toes, your nails, your earlobes, your cells. Be aware of the minute details of your physical form.
- As you begin to connect more with your body, you will feel more relaxed. Intentionally sink deeper into that feeling.
- Allow yourself to let go and consider repeating this phrase over and over: "*I surrender to the wisdom of my higher-self, I am love.*"
- When you are ready to receive, ask the medicine "*Please show me, what do I need to know?*"
- Observe your thoughts and write down whatever comes through without judgment. If you are not able to write, don't worry, you will remember when your journey is finished.
- Allow the medicine to guide you. You will have an internal dialogue that may seem like you're observing a conversation, and you are. It tends to feel like you have three people in your mind—you, your higher-self, and the one observing it all.
- Be inquisitive and allow the medicine to do what it needs to do. Sometimes we don't get the answers right away. Be patient, trust the process.

CHAPTER ELEVEN

Integrating Back Into Everyday Life

More often than not, a deep journey with magic mushrooms can lead to life-changing and life-affirming experiences that will offer you the courage and faith to allow for significant transformations in your life. These changes may come as a surprise to you, however you will likely feel more clear and confident than you ever have before. This is because you have experienced yourself as your true essence, with perspective and awareness that allows you to see your soul's desires without the influence of externalities and values that have likely been imposed on you throughout your life.

You may also find that people in your life who have not had the same experiences with these plant-medicines will not understand what you have been through. They may judge you and your decisions, especially if they are drastic ones. It is very important to stay focused and remain true to yourself and your own authentic discoveries. Now will be a time of complete trust and surrender, challenging at times, but nonetheless you will eventually reap tremendous rewards if you follow your inner guidance and knowing.

If you are at the beginning of your experience with psychoactive plants and fungi, it may be appealing to you to explore multiple master plants, and continue to unpack your subconscious reprogramming with mushrooms. I can't stress enough how crucial it is to always follow this guide and when looking to sit with other plants, be aware that some are not made for solo journeys and definitely need a facilitator, guide or experienced and reputable shaman.

The days and even weeks ahead of your deep mushroom experience may offer you a sense of complete well-being, calmness, euphoria and bliss. During this time, I advise you to make the most out of your awareness by practicing presence, meditation, self-care and self-exploration. Ongoing journaling, writing and forgiveness mantras will be helpful to maintaining this state of peace as you continue to integrate this new found beingness into your life.

Oftentimes it feels like a rebirth when we “awaken” after our psychedelic experiences, and this is not only metaphorical. Your brain has had the opportunity to slow down and rewire old neural nets that fired and wired bad habits and negative emotions and thoughts. Your cells gained an opportunity to reprogram and in many cases you can say a true rebirth has occurred.

A common consensus from participants of magic mushrooms is the overwhelming feeling of love and connectedness to the planet and all its magical beings. Once we are able to access that heart-knowing depth, it is difficult to return to resistance, anger, and self-deprecation. It is only when we disconnect from infinite love that those lower vibrational emotions exist.

This is why many people use magic mushrooms as a regular medicinal ally, to assist in the evolution of their human existence.

Thank you for taking the time to read through this guide. As we deepen our understanding of these sacred plants, we develop new found humility and awe for life. The more we offer reverence to these master teachers, the more we contribute to the healing of the nations.

May your journey be blessed in Bardo and Beyond.

APPENDIX

Safety & Efficacy

Currently, the FDA is exploring the safety and efficacy of using mushrooms as a medication to treat multiple mental health disorders. While the Western Psychiatric frame is limited and reductionist in many ways, these studies have provided some valuable and reassuring information surrounding the safety of mushrooms. In short, the research shows that mushrooms have a very low toxicity profile and are not deeply taxing on the body.[2] In fact, psilocybin is so gentle that it can be used to alleviate the anxiety of those facing grave illnesses without fear of causing harm. The risk of addiction to mushrooms is also very low. When compared to 20 frequently used substances like alcohol, Cocaine and Benzodiazepines, mushrooms had the lowest addiction profile.[3]

With little risk of toxicity or addiction, the most important step to assure the safety of your experience is to make sure that your environment is safe and that you have the support you need to embrace the temporary suppression of your ego-centered experience. While this is one of the most powerful gifts of the mushroom, it also makes it challenging to engage in normal behavior and decision making.

—***Galyn Burke***, Licensed Family & Marriage Therapist

Resources

1. www.timeline.com/with-the-help-of-a-bank-executive-this-mexican-medicine-woman-hipped-america-to-magic-mushrooms-c41f866bbf37

2. www.psilopedia.com/strains

3. www.ncbi.nlm.nih.gov/pmc/articles/PMC5509636/#CR33

www.centerforcm.com

www.maps.org

www.sciencedirect.com/science/article/pii/S0028390818302296

www.synthesisretreat.com/psilocybin-and-ssri-snri-interactionstimeline.com/